The elves' workshop

The clock is ticking and Christmas Eve is fast approaching. Can the elves get all of the toys ready in time?

🐾 Two elves are taking a break and skateboarding around the workshop! Can you spot them?

Can you find...

Snowball fight!

Snow is falling thick and fast and the elves are taking a break from all of their hard work. Did someone say snowball fight? DUCK!

Can you spot the elf wearing a baseball cap?

Can you find...

Where's Santa?

Everyone has dressed up like Santa and it's getting a bit confusing! Where has Santa gone? Can you spot him?

Can you find the penguin wearing sunglasses?

Can you find...

Flying through the sky

Christmas Eve is finally here and Santa is on his way to deliver presents to children around the world. But look out! The sky is chock-a-bloc tonight!

A friendly witch is whizzing around. Can you find her?

Can you find...

Sledding fun!

The toys are made, Santa is on his way and now it's time to have some fun! Skis, skates and sleds at the ready! Let's go! Weeeeee!

A penguin is ice fishing. Can you spot him?

Can you find...

Snowman party

The snowmen are throwing a party to celebrate another successful Christmas. It's time to dance and have some fun!

Can you spot the elf playing the guitar?

Can you find...

Mrs Claus's kitchen

Mrs Claus is cooking up a feast and everything looks so delicious. But some of the gingerbread men are up to no good! What a mess they've made!

Can you spot the elf covered in icing?

Can you find...

Decorating the Christmas tree

Everyone is helping to decorate the Christmas tree. But how will they reach the top? Can you spot the friendly bird helping to get the star in place?

Santa is about to turn on the Christmas lights. Can you spot him?

Can you find...

Christmas carols

Everyone loves Christmas carols, and what better way to celebrate this festive time than singing loud for all to hear!

A cat has joined in the musical fun. Can you spot him?

Can you find...

Christmas morning

Christmas morning has finally arrived and there are presents everywhere! Happy Christmas everyone!

🎁 What has the dog got for Christmas? Can you spot his present?

Can you find...

CHRISTMAS FACTS

Jingle bells
It's reported that the first song preformed in space was Jingle Bells! Astronauts Walter M Schirra Jr. and Thomas P. Stafford brought a harmonica and some sleigh bells all the way to outer space to perform this festive tune!

Reindeer
Santa has nine reindeer that lead his sleigh on Christmas Eve: Dasher, Dancer, Prancer, Vixen, Comet, Cupid, Donner, Blitzen, and of course, Rudolph!

Christmas trees
The tallest Christmas tree ever was almost 68 metres tall and was put up in Seattle, Washington, USA in 1950. How did they manage to put the star on top?

Santa Claus
Santa Claus has lots of different names around the world. Some of his names include Saint Nicholas, Father Christmas, Kris Kringle, Père Noël and de Kerstman.

Presents
If someone really got all of the presents in the Twelve Days of Christmas song they would end up with 364 presents! They would need a lot of wrapping paper!

Giant snowmen
The world's largest snowman was built in Maine in the USA. It measured around 37 metres tall! The people who built the snowman named her 'Olympia SnowWoman'!